F R A N K
L L O Y D
W R I G H T
E A S T
P O R T F O L I O

Text & Photographs by
Thomas A. Heinz

GIBBS·SMITH
P
PUBLISHER

SALT LAKE CITY

96 95 94 93 8 7 6 5 4 3 2 1

This is a Peregrine Smith Book, published by
Gibbs Smith, Publisher
P.O. Box 667
Layton, Utah 84041

Cover photograph: Edgar J. Kaufmann House, Fallingwater, © 1993 by Thomas A. Heinz
Design by J. Scott Knudsen, Park City, Utah
Printed by Regent Publishing Services, Hong Kong

Library of Congress Cataloging–in–Publication Data

Heinz, Thomas A.
    Frank Lloyd Wright portfolio. East/Thomas A. Heinz.
        p.   cm.
    ISBN 0-87905-576-6
    1. Wright, Frank Lloyd, 1867-1959—Criticism and interpretation.
2. Architecture—East (U.S.) I. Title.
NA737.W7H42 1993
720'.92—dc20   93-2194
                                                      CIP

THE DIVERSITY OF WRIGHT'S WORK over the span of his life is well represented in the eastern United States, from the masterful Prairie-era Darwin D. Martin House of Buffalo, built in 1905, to the spiraling Guggenheim Museum of New York City, completed after his death in 1959. The East also contains the most famous of all of Frank Lloyd Wright's designs: Fallingwater. Edgar J. Kaufmann, Sr., commissioned Wright at the suggestion and prodding of his son, Edgar, Jr. It is remarkable that this house ever took shape. Imagine the faith that it took on the part of Kaufmann to hire Wright after he had been without work for about twenty-five years. Even the architectural community discussed Wright in the past tense. Fallingwater and the Johnson Wax Building announced loudly to the world that the creative fires were still burning bright. Fallingwater is not only the most famous, but even as a remote mountain location it is the most visited of Wright's buildings, with nearly 150,000 visitors a year.

When Wright himself stated he was the greatest architect of all time, no one came up with an opposing argument. Wright not only produced more buildings than nearly every architect, but he also produced more unquestionable masterpieces than any single practitioner. The buildings themselves vary so drastically from one another that it is difficult to describe exactly what is the "Wright style." This is because there is no real style, but a design principle that they are all based on. It is the embodiment of Wright's principles that is seen, and the principle of organic design is the thread binding them all together.

The buildings have become well known through the stories of either the quirks of their design or the famous roof leaks. Wright had a lot of faith in what a two-by-four could do. He was constantly trying out new ideas or a different approach to an old one. Given the experimental nature of these designs, it would be expected that there would be some successes as well as some failures. At least in his later work, the Usonian period (1932–59), from the reports of the clients themselves, Wright informed them of the experiments.

There are buildings designed by Frank Lloyd Wright in thirty-six states and in Canada and Japan. Nearly fifty structures are publicly accessible. The best way to begin to appreciate these buildings is to see them in person. Most of the accessible buildings are regularly open for tours.

Thomas A. Heinz
The Guggenheim Museum, New York City
June 1992

DARWIN D. MARTIN HOUSE, SOUTH ELEVATION

L ow-pitched roofs, ribbon windows, simple wall planes, and wide overhangs all make up what has become known as the Prairie House. Mr. Martin's project is one of the best examples of this style. As general manager of the Larkin Company, Martin influenced several other Larkin executives toward Wright designs and the first air-conditioned building: the Larkin Administration Building. Unfortunately, this house was neglected for fifteen years and is in need of careful restoration.

DARWIN D. MARTIN HOUSE, FLOWER URN

Many of Wright's best Prairie houses had unique designs for flower urns. This lime-stone example is nearly six feet wide at the top. The size of these elements often makes it difficult to determine the scale of the urn compared to the building. The urns and the low walls blurred the limits of the house by extending into the landscape. Wright said that it was difficult to tell where the garden ended and the house began.

DARWIN D. MARTIN HOUSE, LIVING ROOM

This furniture display approximates Wright's original arrangement of it and makes an impressive demonstration of his design abilities. The encyclopedia stand on the far right was custom designed for the then-current Encyclopedia Britannica (1904). The quarter-sawn oak of the trim recalls the power and scale of the furnishings. Wright's familiarity with classical design is evident in the use of dentils—small, square, toothlike blocks forming part of the ornamentation—in the head trim that connects all the windows and doors.

LARKIN COMPANY ADMINISTRATION BUILDING, NORTH PIER

This is the last standing element of one of Wright's most important works. Located at the former northwest corner of the site, it is now a parking lot. The building was air-conditioned and used metal office furniture, both technologies that were still in their infancy at the time. The color and scale of this pier gives an impression of the strength of the design for the main portion of the building. The base and cap of the pier are red sandstone. The brickwork is common running bond with colored vertical joints and raked gray mortar horizontal joints. No color photographs of the entire original building have been located. It was demolished in 1950.

Burton Westcott House, South Elevation

Few Prairie-era houses were symmetrical. This example sits on a very large corner lot and was originally designed as a single-family dwelling, but it has been subdivided into apartments, which obscures a complete understanding of the spatial flow. The lower level is the living room and the upper story contains the bedrooms. The gray stucco appears to be the original color and fits in well with the red shingle roof. The entry is on the right, close to the street.

BURTON WESTCOTT HOUSE, FLOWER URN

I n contrast to the Darwin D. Martin House urn (p. 6), this urn is oriented vertically and stands over six feet tall and is about the same in the width. As with all dirt-containing vessels at Wright houses, there is a pipe drain to allow water to escape. If water were to be trapped, it could freeze and split the bowl. The Westcott urns are the largest at any Wright house. They also throw off the sense of scale; one is not quite sure how big or small things are. Compare the size of the urn with the stairs just to the left of it. These urns are sited about halfway between the front street and the house.

E. E. BOYNTON HOUSE, WEST FRONT

Often overshadowed by the work in nearby Buffalo, this is one of the great designs in Wright's Prairie era. The living room is just behind the porch on the right, with the dining room to the left in the lower level. The dining room once overlooked a large garden, but a later house was built, squeezing the Wright-designed house a bit. The dining room itself is a story-and-a-half high, with a lower breakfast area toward the garden. The simple art-glass patterns of the first floor appear to be inverted when used on the second floor.

E. E. Boynton House, Dining Room Ceiling Light

T his is the left, or west, unit of a trio of ceiling lights that are above the main dining table. The opposite unit is the same pattern but reversed, and the central unit contains a simpler pattern. It is unusual for Wright to include wood members as a part of the pattern. Regularly, wood would be used only as the frame of the art glass, both in ceiling lights and windows. The small fields of checkerboards are comprised of one-quarter-inch squares of glass bounded by zinc cames. The largest of the metal cames is an inch wide.

WALTER DAVIDSON HOUSE, LIVING ROOM

One of several similar designs—including the Isabel Roberts House, Frank Baker House, and the demolished Oscar Steffans House, all of the Chicago area—this house is light and airy. Through the use of several structural innovations, the room has only one roof cross-tie. The overhangs act as trusses cantilevering the roof joist to the ridge. The folds in the walls help to stabilize it.

FRANCIS LITTLE SUMMER HOUSE, RECONSTRUCTION, LIVING ROOM

The broad walls afforded views over the south lawn and Lake Minnetonka to the north on its original site in west suburban Minneapolis. The author was the restoration architect for the museum when it was reconstructed in the American Wing at the Metropolitan Museum of Art in the early 1980s. There are six sets each of ceiling lights, clerestory windows, and casement windows in the lower bays. Wright plays a visual trick on the observer by increasing the width of each unit of window or ceiling light from the bay to the ceiling. As the largest residential interior in Wright's career, it is now the largest period room in the world. The couch on the left is the original from the Robie House in Chicago and was never in the Little House in Minnesota.

EDGAR KAUFMANN HOUSE, FALLINGWATER, DOWNSTREAM ELEVATION

E ven against the white snow and the cool blue sky, the warmth of the house is evident. The red paint on the window mullions creates a contrast with the natural materials that make up the rest of the house. At one time early in the work, Wright suggested using gold leaf on the exposed concrete. His idea was that the house would then be even more reflective of the changing light conditions in this little valley.

EDGAR KAUFFMAN HOUSE, FALLINGWATER, GUEST HOUSE AND CANOPY

The guest house, built several years after the main house, is "joined" to the main house by a canopy which protects the curved stone stairway. An original design of William Wesley Peters, Wright's son-in-law and second in command, the canopy is supported by thin metal posts at the outside only. It appears to float without support on the inside edge. It is actually a folded concrete compression ring. The guest house itself contains a guest living room, bath and bedroom on the right, with the servants' quarters on the second level. The carports are below the second level on the far left.

EDGAR KAUFMANN HOUSE, FALLINGWATER, INTERIOR VIEW

This unusual evening view illuminates all three levels of the house and the guest house at the top. Seeing the master bedroom (center) and the guest room (right) on the second level gives a clear sense of the continuity Wright intended.

EDGAR KAUFMANN HOUSE, FALLINGWATER, THIRD LEVEL EAST

Standing at Edgar, Jr.'s, bed looking down the third-level hallway and into the library, one gets a sense of the light/dark contrasts that make this building so intriguing to visitors and residents. The library was originally to be Edgar, Jr.'s, bedroom, but he preferred the smaller, more open niche at the opposite (north) end of the floor.

Edgar Kaufmann House, Fallingwater, Living Room

The rock that rises out of the floor at the fireplace extends well into bedrock and anchors the entire house actually, and here figuratively. The uneven flagstones recall the streambed below. The shine recalls the water flowing over the rocks and is a result of the polish of a Johnson's wax. The large metal pot was intended for warming mulled wine but proved too difficult and too large to be useful. It is similar to the one that hangs in the dining room fireplace at Herbert Johnson's house, known as Wingspread, in Racine, Wisconsin. Metal bands replace the wood trim bands Wright used in his Prairie houses.

KAUFMANN HOUSE, FALLINGWATER, LIVING ROOM FURNITURE

T he arrangement of this furniture grouping is taken from a layout that Wright drew. It is not usually seen this way during the tours. The composition is quite reminiscent of the house design's overlapping cantilevered edges, and it recalls the cascading of the water down the stream and over the waterfall. The Kaufmanns lived with a much less formal grouping. The long stretches of wide, built-in seating were often used for sleeping guests, and this room alone could accommodate at least four adults.

EDGAR KAUFMANN HOUSE, FALLINGWATER, VERTICAL WINDOWS

*I*n contrast to the horizontality of the concrete balconies, this set of steel windows opens the vertical corner of the house. When all are open, the windows completely eliminate the corner, as shown in the single window at the center of the first and second floors. The concrete floors taper at the window and only contact the metal mullions, obscuring the different levels. At the right side of the windows, the glass dies into the stone without any metal to receive it. This allows the plane of the stone to appear uninterrupted from the outside to the inside. One of Wright's major ideas was to obscure the line between inside and out. This is one of his most successful examples.

POPE/LEIGHY HOUSE, SOUTH ELEVATION

T he house was threatened by the construction of a major highway and was moved to its present location, but the highway was never built. The original site was flat and the house fit well on that site. The combination of sets of doors and high windows allows for rising heat to escape and provides soothing breezes in the hot summers. Wright seemed to have a talent for coming up with natural solutions to enhance human comfort.

POPE/LEIGHY HOUSE, LIVING ROOM

The concept of concentrated window areas and dark, windowless stretches of wall is much like a cave, a secure place that can be inhabited singularly or in a group. The acoustics in this room are excellent for both conversation and music, as with most of Wright's residential interiors. The pattern of the row of vertical fretwork screens is a part of the larger design at the top of the wall above the bookcase. The seating on the lower left side is actually a line of free-standing armless chairs that can be arranged according to the group dynamics of the moment.

POPE/LEIGHY HOUSE, BEDROOM WINDOWS, CUT FRETWORK SCREEN

Over his career, Wright spoke of light screens. They would modulate the light and at the same time provide privacy for the interior, eliminating the need for draperies. Stained glass filled this function in an artful manner early in his career, and later he developed the cut fretwork screen for the same purpose. The carpenters on the job were able to do the finish work on these fret wood screens.

ISADORE J. ZIMMERMAN HOUSE, NORTH FRONT ENTRY

The plain, simple roof protects the light-colored concrete-block window line. The partly exposed rock is a natural highlight at the front door. The public side of the house presents a secure front, in contrast to the open yard side.

ISADORE J. ZIMMERMAN HOUSE, LIVING ROOM

The long stretch of bench seating is opposite the large windows overlooking the backyard. The simple up-lighting in the deck over the seats provides a pleasant, diffused lighting, while the down-lights at the brick columns and in the underside of the deck provide accent and reading light.

ISAAC NEWTON HAGAN HOUSE, WEST FRONT ENTRY

A s with the Zimmerman House, this entry is quite protected. The glass sidelights make the entry open and inviting. Hagan's company produced the premium ice cream of the region. He was a bit embarrassed at being named Isaac Newton, and everyone knew him only as "I. N."

ISAAC NEWTON HAGAN HOUSE, KITCHEN

This tall a space would be unexpected in such an apparently low structure. Without access to an exterior wall, the full ceiling skylight still makes the room appear bright and sunny. The height of the room traps cooking smoke and odors.

ROBERT L. WRIGHT HOUSE, SOUTH ELEVATION

Catherine and Frank Lloyd Wright had six children. Their youngest was Robert Llewellyn, who became a prominent attorney in Washington. Robert took the lead of his older brother, David, and asked his father for a house design. The result was quite unique, even for Wright. A football in plan, it has the typical ribbon window elevation of most of the houses from Wright's Usonian period (1932–59). Even some of the furniture has the football shape. It sounds odd, but, as usual with Wright's furniture, it is very comfortable and soothing.

GUGGENHEIM MUSEUM, WEST ELEVATION

Wright began this design in 1943 and it took nearly fifteen years to complete. During that time, the large spiral exhibit space was shifted from the north side to the south side. Because the original buiding design was so controversial, the city planners and building code administrators held up the construction until the late 1950s. Wright was able to oversee most of the construction before he passed away in April 1959. The large gray block on the left is an addition that opened in late 1992 and is connected to the spiral galleries of the main exhibit space. The design and construction of the new addition caused nearly as much controversy as did the original building.

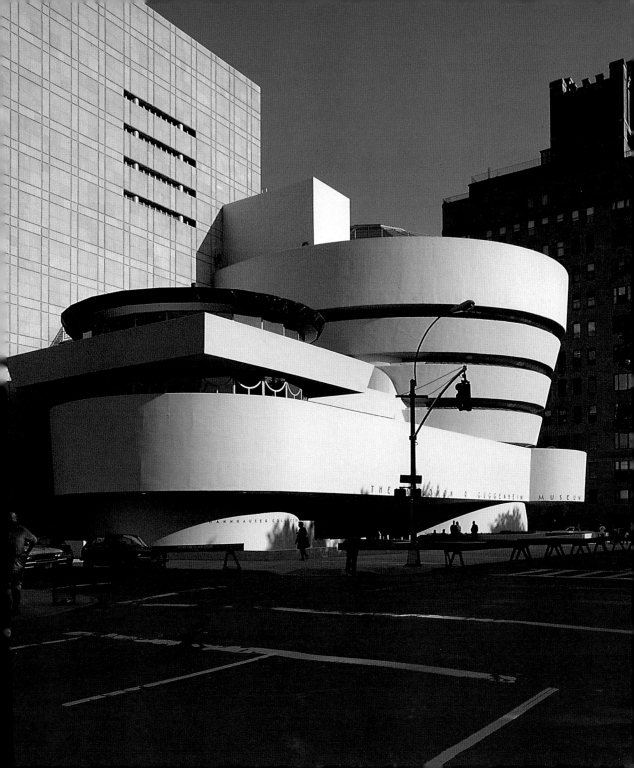

GUGGENHEIM MUSEUM, INTERIOR RAMP

The interior is a spiral helix beginning at the elevator and ending at the elliptical pool at the floor. On the exterior, the bands appear to be horizontal. Visitors have an easy trip down the ramp and are able to see the entire collection on the way down.

BETH SHOLOM SYNAGOGUE, WEST ELEVATION

Wright was constantly exploring the possibilities of different geometries. He made several attempts at a triangular scheme before this successful structure. The shape is an abstraction of a quartz crystal. A similar but much smaller structure was designed for the Kaufmann's Rhododendron Chapel, and again on an immense scale as Steel Cathedral for New York.

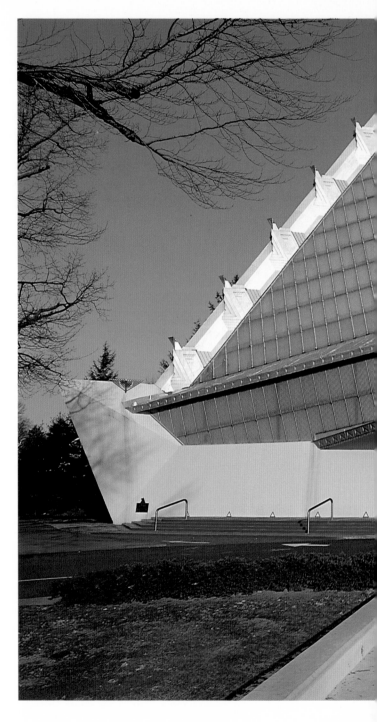

BETH SHOLOM SYNAGOGUE, LIGHT FINIAL

T he light finials extend the entire length of the three structural ribs that define the interior auditorium space. They modify the impact of these members by breaking up the surface and the edges. They do not light up as shown in Wright's famous night rendering of the synagogue. The entire design reminds one of the early Middle East pyramids with the torches at each level along the corners.

Beth Sholom Synagogue, Interior

The gray roof becomes quite golden, even on overcast days. The interior appears twice as big as the exterior. The design of the Ark and the massive Monolith is perfectly proportioned for the space. It is well integrated and does not feel like it was plopped down in a warehouse. This space is entered from below rather than by walking directly through a door. Because one cannot see the whole space at one view, there is a sense of anticipation and drama.

❦ Beth Sholom Synagogue, 1954
Old York Road
Elkins Park, Pennsylvania
pages 58, 60, 62

E. E. Boynton House, 1908
16 East Boulevard
Rochester, New York
pages 16, 18

Walter Davidson House, 1908
57 Tillinghast
Buffalo, New York
page 20

❦ Guggenheim Museum,
  1943–59
1071 5th Avenue at 88th Street
New York, New York
pages 54, 56

Isaac Newton Hagan House,
  1954
Connelsville Road
Ohiopyle, Pennsylvania
pages 48, 50

❦ Edgar J. Kaufmann House,
  Fallingwater, 1936
Route 381
Mill Run, Pennsylvania
pages 24, 26, 28, 30, 32, 34,
  36, cover
© Western Pennsylvania
Conservancy, photographs by
Thomas A. Heinz

❦ Larkin Company
  Administration Building
  (demolished), 1904
680 Seneca Street
Buffalo, New York
page 10

❦ Francis Little House,
  (reconstruction), 1913
Metropolitan Museum of Art
Fifth Avenue at 82nd Street
New York, New York
page 22

❦ Darwin D. Martin House,
  1904
125 Jewett Parkway
Buffalo, New York
pages 4, 6, 8

❦ Pope/Leighy House, 1940
Woodlawn Plantation
Mount Vernon, Virginia
pages 38, 40, 42

Burton Westcott House, 1907
1340 East High Street
Springfield, Ohio
pages 12, 14

Robert Llewellyn Wright House,
  1953
7927 Deepwell Drive
Bethesda, Maryland
page 52

❦ Isadore J. Zimmerman House,
  1950
223 Heather Street
Manchester, New Hampshire
page 44, 46

❦ These properties are open for public tours.